HOW TO PROTECT ENDANGERED ANIMALS

Animal Book Age 10 | Children's Animal Books

BABY PROFESSOR
EDUCATION KIDS

Speedy Publishing LLC
40 E. Main St. #1156
Newark, DE 19711
www.speedypublishing.com
Copyright 2017

All Rights reserved. No part of this book may be reproduced or used in any way or form or by any means whether electronic or mechanical, this means that you cannot record or photocopy any material ideas or tips that are provided in this book

In this book, we're going to talk about how animals become endangered and how to protect them from going extinct. So, let's get right to it!

WHAT IS AN ENDANGERED ANIMAL?

Every species on Earth is unique and valuable. Unfortunately, there are many events that can cause an animal species to die out. If a type of animal dies out completely it goes "extinct," which means we'll never see it on Earth again. Some animals are extinct in the wild because there are only a few of them left in zoos.

Once a population of animals is at risk to possibly die out, we say that it's "endangered."

In the movie, Jurassic Park, scientists take DNA from fossils and recreate dinosaurs that went extinct about 65 million years ago. Someday, it may be possible for this to happen, but for now it's just science fiction. Once animals or plants are gone, they're gone forever.

WHAT CAUSES ANIMALS TO BECOME ENDANGERED?

There are many types of events that can cause animals to become endangered or extinct. These can happen in single events or there can be several factors all at once.

NATURAL DISASTERS

Before people evolved on Earth, there were natural disasters that caused animals to become endangered or extinct. Sometimes these changes occurred over thousands of years, but, at other times, the events were so devastating that the extinctions happened soon afterwards.

For example, many believe that the extinction of the dinosaurs was caused by an enormous meteorite that hit the Earth. The impact was so strong, that clouds of dust polluted the atmosphere and blocked the sun's rays from getting to Earth, causing climate change.

Polar Bear

HUMAN INTERACTION

Natural disasters still have an impact on animal species. However, in most cases animals are becoming endangered or extinct due to interference by man. More and more people are living on Earth. As we take up more space and use resources, animal habitats are disappearing.

If animals can't adapt, then they become endangered or go extinct. Many scientists believe that the rate of extinction is increasing beyond what would occur naturally because of human interference.

Bisons

OVERHUNTING FOR FOOD OR BODY PARTS

When the Europeans first came to North America there were bison in record numbers. Millions filled up the plains and when they ran they sounded like thunder. The bison were overhunted and started to die out. They couldn't reproduce fast enough to recover their population. A few animals survived and conservationists stepped in to help them. Now they aren't endangered anymore.

Overhunting is particularly dangerous on islands. Islands sometimes have species that don't live anywhere else, so if they are overhunted, they die out quickly.

It's not just overhunting for food that is a problem. Sometimes animals are overhunted for their fur, bones, feathers, or horns. African elephants were being killed in record numbers for their ivory horns until they became endangered. They are protected by laws now, however poachers are still killing them for ivory in some areas.

African Elephants

LOSS OF HABITATS

One of the problems that is causing animals to become endangered is loss of habitats. As humans build and develop land, there's less and less space for animals to occupy the types of environments that are natural for them. When large areas are cleared to grow crops for people, it throws the whole food chain out of balance and many types of animals become endangered or die out.

POLLUTION

Another factor is industrial pollution. As waterways are poisoned and one species dies out, other species that depend on that species for food die out as well, which affects all the animals in that environment.

Lionfish

NON-NATIVE SPECIES

If a species gets introduced into an environment where it wasn't living before, then it's not native to that environment and can cause a lot of trouble. For example, lionfish were introduced into the waters off the coast of Florida from someone who dumped them out from an aquarium. Lionfish weren't native in those waterways and now they are killing other fish in record numbers.

Since they weren't part of the environment before, they have no natural predators to keep their population under control. Human beings are not always at fault, but in most cases we are as we bring animals or plants into environments far away from their native homes.

Eastern grey squirrels are invasive species in Europe

HOW CAN WE PREVENT ANIMALS FROM BECOMING ENDANGERED?

We can't prevent all extinctions. We don't have control over huge natural disasters. However, we can change our own behavior. Long-term conservation techniques, such as putting protection laws in place, make a difference. Working to keep our air and water clean helps animals stay healthy and helps us too.

Making sure that critical habitats are preserved is important as well. Using synthetic materials for medicines instead of overhunting animals for that purpose prevents animals from becoming at risk for extinction.

Hawksbill Sea Turtle

TEN WAYS YOU CAN HELP ENDANGERED SPECIES

Everyone can participate in helping conservationists to keep animals from becoming endangered. Here are ten things you can do to help out:

1. Do some research to find out which animals in your area are endangered. Once you know, share this information with your family and friends.

Giant Panda

Manatee

People are much more aware of what they do that hurts animals, once they understand how important and interesting these animals are. The Earth provides us with water, land, and resources for food and medicine. If we're careful about how these resources are used, then they will continue to be there for us.

2. Talk to your parents about donating to a conservationist organization. Most of these environmental activist groups are nonprofits and they need funds to continue to do their valuable work conserving animals and plants for the future.

3. Visit your local zoo, park, or wildlife refuge. One of the best ways to help animals and plants is to protect where they live. By visiting these areas you are supplying valuable funds environmentalists need to continue their work. You and your parents can also volunteer at these nature centers and help in a more direct way. Do some research online to locate the nearest zoo, national park, or wildlife refuge close to where you live.

4. Reduce the impact of your home on the environment. Make sure that garbage cans have secure lids so that wild animals won't eat things they shouldn't eat. Keep pet food inside for the same reason and make sure any pet doors are locked up at night so that wild animals don't get inside your home.

Clean bird baths on a regular basis so that insects won't breed there and transmit disease. Position window decals on your outside

windows so birds won't fly into them. Birds die in the millions each year from crashing into residential and business windows.

5. Make sure the plants you position in your landscape areas are correct for the environment. Frequently, non-native plants have been planted because someone liked the way they looked and wanted them in their landscaped areas.

Kudzu covered field

These non-native plants have then multiplied and taken over vast areas. For example, kudzu was a plant native to Asia. It was brought over to the United States in 1876 as an ornamental bush and has now spread over millions of acres of land. It smothers other plants under a blanket of leaves and they die. Kudzu is hard to get rid of.

6. Keep pesticides to a minimum and use natural products instead. Pesticides are toxic to soil. This toxicity impacts the food chain at every level. Amphibians are dying out in record numbers since they are very sensitive to these poisons.

   When amphibians like frogs and toads become poisoned, it impacts the birds of prey like hawks and owls that eat them. Do some research to find natural alternatives that keep your lawn healthy, but don't hurt animals or plants.

7. Recycle and buy products from sustainable sources. Most people buy recycled paper and most families in the United States recycle packaging they buy. If you think about ways to recycle, reduce, and reuse every day, you'll be helping the environment and this ultimately helps animals and plants.

Pay attention to the things you buy to make sure that when they are created it doesn't have an impact on the environment. For example, items made from palm oil mean that forests were cut down for palm plantations. These forests are vital habitats for tigers, which is an endangered species.

Palm Plantation

Tortoise

8. Don't buy products that were made from endangered species. Sometimes souvenirs in foreign countries are made from animals that are nearing extinction. Tortoise shell, coral, and ivory are some examples.

9. Convince your parents to slow down while driving. Many people and animals are killed every year when animals are hit by cars. These accidents and the loss of both human and animal life could be prevented by slower, more careful driving.

10. Protect the habitats of wildlife. Scientists have reported that the best way to protect species is to make sure their natural homes are safe. Just like humans, they need food and shelter.

Do your part to protect these habitats by supporting wildlife sanctuaries and open space in your area.

Red Panda

Awesome! Now you know more about how to protect endangered animals. You can find more Animal books from Baby Professor by searching the website of your favorite book retailer.

Printed in Great Britain
by Amazon